£2.95

THIS BOOK
BELONGS TO :—

Name ....

Address ....

....

....

Printed and Published in Great Britain by D. C. Thomson & Co., Ltd.,
185 Fleet Street, London, EC4A 2HS.

GINGER

THERE'S UNCLE GEORGE. I HAVEN'T SEEN HIM FOR AGES.

YOO-HOO! UNCLE GEORGE!

Suddenly —

SOLD TO THE YOUNG MAN AT THE DOOR.

EH? WHAT? OH, NO! IT'S AN AUCTION SALE.

BAH! I HAD TO PAY A POUND FOR THIS CHAIR!

Just then —

HEY, GINGER! LET ME BORROW YOUR CHAIR!

ER — OKAY!

And —

NOW I CAN GET MY CAT DOWN!

WOWEE! HE PAID FOR THE LOAN OF THE CHAIR.

Raise the alarm! The Lads are at a Health Farm!

the BADD LADS

Blindman's-buff leaves the twins in a huff!

BABY CROCKETT

POST EARLY FOR CHRISTMAS

WHY DO YOU SEND CHRISTMAS CARDS, MUM?

TO LET FRIENDS YOU HAVEN'T SEEN FOR A LONG TIME KNOW THAT YOU ARE THINKING ABOUT THEM!

ME COULD DO THAT!

LET ME SEE...

WHAT A PILE OF CARDS YOU'RE SENDING. ARE THEY TO GRAN, AUNTIE FLO, COUSIN SANDY?

NO!

FRED'S PET MOUSE!

SALLY'S BUDGIE!

TOMMY'S FROG!

WILLIE'S RAT!

ANNE'S PUP!

COLONEL BLINK

Grit in the eye makes a grown man cry!

The NUMSKULLS

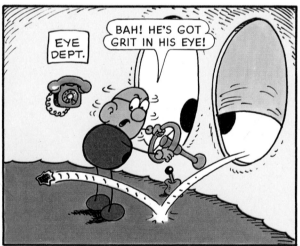

AH, WELL! THE WATER HAS WASHED AWAY THAT BIT OF GRIT.

Soon after—

OUR MAN'S EYES ARE NEEDING SOME SORT OF PROTECTION, BRAINY.

HM! YOU COULD BE RIGHT, BLINKY.

BRAIN DEPT.

THIS SHOULD DO THE TRICK.

GO AND BUY SUN-GLASSES

SUGGESTION BOX

So—

I'LL TAKE THESE, PLEASE.

But outside—

GOSH! I CAN'T SEE VERY WELL.

I CAN'T SEE A THING. I'LL PHONE BRAINY AND TELL HIM THE SUN-SPECS ARE NO USE.

But—

BAH! THE PHONE'S OUT OF ORDER.

Life is rough for the cowardly Tuff!

TUFF AND TINY

In the jungle —

THIS IS A GREAT GAME OF TENNIS!

Then —

COO! MY TAIL'S REALLY WARM ALL OF A SUDDEN!

EEK! A SNAKE! WHAT A SHOCK!

THAT'S BECAUSE I'M AN ELECTRICITY 'PYTHON'! HEE-HEE!

GET IT OFF, TINY!

DON'T WORRY, TUFF! I'LL RESCUE YOU!

I'LL SOON GET RID OF THAT SNAKE!

THINGS HOTTING UP FOR YOU, ARE THEY, SNAKEY?

OOYAH!

Several days later —

AH! ISN'T IT NICE AND PEACEFUL NOW?

IT SURE IS!

SHERIFF'S OFFICE

Just then —

HUH! THERE'S NO FUN IN THE VALLEY NOW. WE MIGHT AS WELL LEAVE!

At the same time —

I HATE TO SAY IT, BUT I'M MISSING THOSE PESKY HILLYS.

HEAD FOR THE HILLS, HILLYS.

LET'S GO, BILLYS!

CRASH!

WHAT . . ?

EEK!

WHEE! NICE TO BUMP INTO YOU AGAIN.

And soon —

BANG! BANG! CRACK! BANG!

OH, NO! THEY'VE STARTED AGAIN!

AH, WELL! AT LEAST WE GOT A COUPLE OF DAYS' PEACE!

SHERIFF'

Brainy has a hunch how to make a castle for the Bunch!

THE Banana Bunch

...AND THE WALLS IN THIS PART OF THE CASTLE ARE TEN FEET THICK!

COO!

Castle Flint

NEVER IN ITS HISTORY HAS CASTLE FLINT BEEN CAPTURED.

THAT WAS GREAT! I WISH WE LIVED IN A CASTLE!

Back at the hut—

LET'S TURN OUR HUT INTO A CASTLE!

FIRST, WE CAN MAKE OUR DOOR INTO A DRAWBRIDGE!

OH, DEAR! I EXPECTED IT TO FALL THE OTHER WAY!

AARGH!

NEXT, WE'LL DIG A MOAT ROUND OUR HUT!

The tiny mite is looking for a fight!

Puzzle

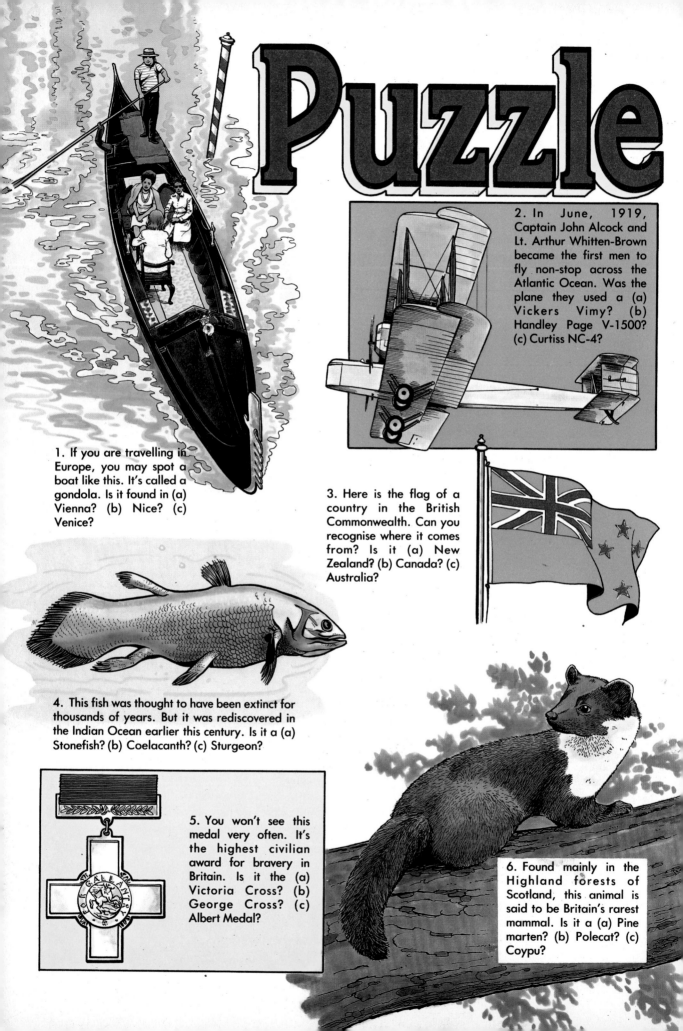

1. If you are travelling in Europe, you may spot a boat like this. It's called a gondola. Is it found in (a) Vienna? (b) Nice? (c) Venice?

2. In June, 1919, Captain John Alcock and Lt. Arthur Whitten-Brown became the first men to fly non-stop across the Atlantic Ocean. Was the plane they used a (a) Vickers Vimy? (b) Handley Page V-1500? (c) Curtiss NC-4?

3. Here is the flag of a country in the British Commonwealth. Can you recognise where it comes from? Is it (a) New Zealand? (b) Canada? (c) Australia?

4. This fish was thought to have been extinct for thousands of years. But it was rediscovered in the Indian Ocean earlier this century. Is it a (a) Stonefish? (b) Coelacanth? (c) Sturgeon?

5. You won't see this medal very often. It's the highest civilian award for bravery in Britain. Is it the (a) Victoria Cross? (b) George Cross? (c) Albert Medal?

6. Found mainly in the Highland forests of Scotland, this animal is said to be Britain's rarest mammal. Is it a (a) Pine marten? (b) Polecat? (c) Coypu?

Pics

7. This ship was built to take Captain Scott on his Antarctic explorations of 1901-1904. The vessel is now on display in its home port of Dundee where it was built. Is it the (a) Endurance? (b) Terra Nova? (c) Discovery?

8. Superb at catching fish, this bird of prey is so rare in Britain, that its nest is often guarded to make sure that the eggs are not stolen. Is it an (a) Arctic tern? (b) Auk? (c) Osprey?

9. The panda is one of the world's favourite animals. But its future is in danger because it requires a special kind of food. Is that food (a) Eucalyptus leaves? (b) Bamboo shoots? (c) Sugar cane leaves?

10. The largest lizard in the world is the Komodo Monitor found on several Indonesian Islands. Do you know how big these creatures grow? Is it (a) 8 feet long? (b) 12 feet long? (c) 5 feet long?

11. The highest speed ever recorded by a steam locomotive is 126 miles per hour. Was the name of the locomotive the (a) Flying Scotsman? (b) Mallard? (c) Britannia?

ANSWERS
1 (c). 2 (a). 3 (a). 4 (b).
5 (b). 6 (a). 7 (c). 8 (c).
9 (b). 10 (a). 11 (b).

JOE SOAP

JOE BROWN was known as Joe Soap by the people of Sudbury. You see, he was always blowing bubbles made by his grandfather, a real crackpot inventor. One day, Joe was playing cricket in the garden.

I'LL BET YOU CAN'T HIT THIS ONE, JOE!

OH, NO? WATCH THIS, GRANDAD!

OO-ER! I'VE BROKEN THE BAT!

I'LL MIX UP SOMETHING TO STICK THE PIECES TOGETHER.

THANKS, GRANDAD!

Soon —

THIS WILL MAKE JOE'S BAT AS GOOD AS NEW.

Meanwhile —

I'LL PRACTISE MY BOWLING WHILE I'M WAITING FOR GRANDAD!

And —

MADE IT!

DID YOU DISTURB ALL THOSE BATS?

ER — YES! I DID!

WELL, YOU'LL GET A REWARD. WE DIDN'T KNOW HOW TO GET RID OF THEM.

WHEE! A REWARD! WE'LL BE ABLE TO BUY A NEW BAT AND STILL HAVE PLENTY LEFT OVER.

Later —

THANKS FOR BUYING THE BAT, GRANDAD! NOW WHAT WOULD YOU LIKE TO EAT . . . A STEAK?

ER . . . NO "STAKES" FOR ME! THEY'D GIVE ME HEARTBURN OR SOMETHING!

HUNGRY HOSS

A gorilla trap set by the clever Sid chap!

YOUNG SID

THE COPPER'S KID

PAW, MAW and PORKY

THE YOUTH CLUB HUT NEEDS REPAIR. BUT WE DON'T HAVE THE CASH!

SLOBBER!

WE'LL START OUR OWN POP GROUP!

I'LL FETCH MY GUITAR! PEOPLE WILL PAY PLENTY TO HEAR US PLAY!

INTERESTING. VERY INTERESTING.

Back home—

WHAT'S UP, PORKY?

I'M GOING TO RAISE CASH FOR THE YOUTH CLUB!

I WONDER IF I CAN HELP!

Shortly—

YOU KNOW, THEY AREN'T BAD—

BLARE! HOWL! DRONE!

—THEY'RE AWFUL!

D

SMiFFY

ARE YOU GOING TO STAY WITH ME WHILE MUMMY GOES SHOPPING, PETER?

I'LL JUST GET HIS PLAYPEN!

I'VE ORDERED A BAG OF CEMENT FROM THE IRONMONGER. GO AND FETCH IT FOR ME, SMIFFY.

IT'LL BE HEAVY! HOW WILL I GET IT HOME, DAD?

YOU CAN WHEEL IT HOME IN PETER'S PRAM!

WHAT? ME PUSH A PRAM? AW, DAD!

And —

HO-HO! LOOK AT SMIFFY! WHAT A SOP!

YOU'VE LOST YOUR DOLLY! THE PRAM'S EMPTY! HA-HA!

At the ironmonger's —

PHEW! WHAT A WEIGHT!

BAH! IF I CAN GET OVER THE BROW OF THIS HILL, IT'S DOWNHILL ALL THE WAY HOME FROM THERE.

CEMENT

A battle to see what to watch on T.V.

POP, DICK and HARRY!

One Saturday morning—

HEY! THERE'S A GREAT COWBOY FILM ON THE TELLY THIS MORNING, HARRY, BUT POP'S GARDENING PROGRAMME'S ON AT THE SAME TIME.

WE'LL JUST MAKE SURE THAT POP STAYS IN BED. HERE'S WHAT WE'LL DO!

And so—

GRUB'S THE ONLY THING THAT'LL TAKE POP'S MIND OFF THE TELLY!

WHAT'S THIS? BREAKFAST IN BED? BUT IT ISN'T MY BIRTHDAY!

HUH! IT ISN'T GOING TO TAKE HIM LONG TO FINISH THAT LOT! HE'LL GET UP SOON!

NOW TRY PLAN TWO! REMEMBER WHAT I TOLD YOU?

DON'T GET UP, POP! I WANT TO READ YOU A BEDTIME STORY!

WHAT? IN THE MORNING? DON'T BE RIDICULOUS!

BESIDES! THERE'S A GARDENING PROGRAMME I WANT TO SEE ON THE TELLY!

BEEZER

SHREDUL
NIPTSR
ALIJEVN
SIDSUC
MERAHM

Ginger would like to take part in some of the sports events at the gala. But the names of the events are all mixed up. Can you help him to unscramble the names?

Saucy Sue has sold 51 programmes more than Mugsy who has sold 6 less than Porky. P.C. 99 has sold 2 more than Porky and Mugsy put together. If Mugsy has sold 23, how many programmes altogether have been sold?

The sack race is about to start — but who is taking part in it?

The spoons for the egg and spoon race have gone missing. See if you can find all 6 of them scattered on these pages.

They're under starter's orders for the wheelbarrow race — but our artist has made 6 mistakes in this picture. What are they?

TEEZERS

How many objects beginning with the letter 'B' can you find for sale on this bric-a-brac stand?

BRIC-A-BRAC

1 2 3 4

5 6

Boss would like to pinch a couple of cups for his collection, but he doesn't want them to be the same. In fact, only 2 are exactly alike. Can you spot them?

Dopey has tied people's legs together for the three-legged race. Who is running with whom?

Young Sid has landed in trouble at the pole vault. Can you help him to get down to the sandpit by turning POLE to SAND in four moves, and by changing one letter at a time to make a new word?

POLE

_____

_____

_____

SAND

ANSWERS

POLE VAULT — Pole; sole; sale; sane; sand — is one way.

THREE-LEGGED RACE — Smiffy and Baby; Fingers and Pop; Harry and Paw; Tuff and Tiny.

SPOONS — On leg of notice board; in bush; on copper's helmet; in Boss's pocket; on bric-a-brac stall; in sandpit.

SACK RACE — Knuck; Mo; Wolfie; Dick.

OBJECTS — Balloon; bird; brolly; ball; boat; book; bat; bottle; broom.

CUPS — 3 and 5 are the same.

Brainy's waistcoat; Blinky has one welly on. Fatty's; Tiny facing the wrong way; one odd button on

pistol; square wheel on Lanky's barrow; no wheel on

WHEELBARROW—Bow and arrow instead of starting

PROGRAMMES — 180.

SCRAMBLED NAMES — Hurdles; sprint; javelin; discus; hammer.

Baby is found to be be muscle-bound!

BABY CROCKETT

E

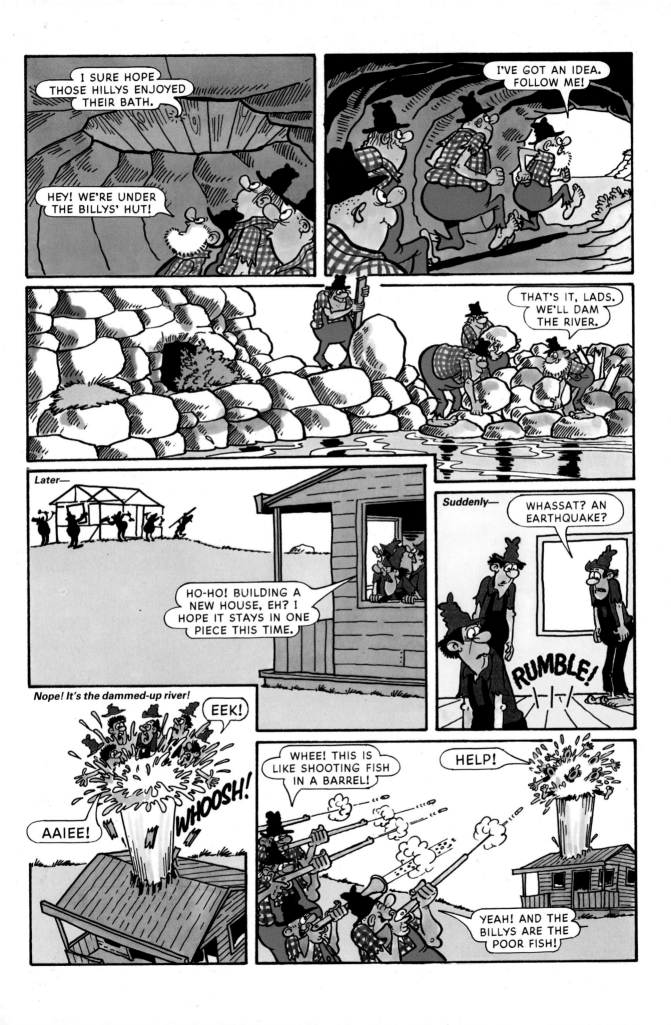

BABY CROCKETT'S

Time marches on!

HOPE TO REACH NEW HEIGHTS THIS YEAR!

Another birthday

HOPE TO HAVE A WHALE OF A TIME!

Seeing it's my birthday party—

BIRTHDAY GREETINGS

Me's really growing up!

Putting my best foot forward on my birthday

Hope I'll be excused baffs!

It's my Birthday— Hope to—

Have a good smile!

Scrapper needs a nap after a scrap!

HUNGRY HOSS

But—

Inside—

Meanwhile—

Then—

And—

Beware of Wolfie's new car — It can be controlled from afar!

PAW, MAW AND PORKY

A powerboat dash to escape with some cash!

The NUMSKULLS

EYE DEPT.

I'M NOT WATCHING THAT RUBBISH. I'M OFF FOR A BATH.

I'LL RUN THE WATER WHILE I GET CHANGED.

Then—

BAH! I'VE SEEN THIS BEFORE!

I'LL TELL OUR MAN TO CHANGE IT OVER AGAIN. I MIGHT AS WELL LET BLINKY SEE BLACK BEAUTY.

EYE DEPT.

So—

BRAIN DEPT

SWITCH BACK TO BLACK BEAUTY

SUGGESTION BOX

And—

I THINK I'LL WATCH BLACK BEAUTY INSTEAD.

OH, GOOD!

NOW MO IS HANGING AROUND, I'LL MAKE A FORTUNE WITH HER MANICURE SET.

HEY!

Much later—

GRR! TIME FOR REVENGE!

AHA! THERE HE IS!

MO'S MUGSY'S MANICURE SERVICE

MUGSY! I'VE GOT A CUSTOMER FOR YOU!

GREAT!

AH, YES! PLEASE BE FILING MY NAILS!

EH?

OH, NO! HE MEANS A BED OF NAILS!

HA-HA! ONLY 1000 LEFT!